EXPERIENCE Modern ISRAEL

Teacher's Lesson Plan Manual

By Nathan Weiner

Plus Modern Israel Online

Project Editors: Beth Panitz, Dena Neusner
Design: Annemarie Redmond

Springfield, New Jersey
ISBN: 978-0-87441-801-9 • Printed in the U.S.A.

Behrman House Publishers
www.behrmanhouse.com
www.behrmanhouse.com/EMI

Contents

INTRODUCTION

STRUCTURE OF *EXPERIENCE MODERN ISRAEL*

Experience Modern Israel helps students in grades 5-7 gain a meaningful understanding of modern Israeli culture. The text explores Israel's origins, its historical and religious significance to the Jewish people, and the internal and external challenges facing the Jewish state.

Because many students have never been to Israel, they do not realize that it is a vibrant, modern nation. *Experience Modern Israel* provides a real-life glimpse into the country through lively text and engaging, experiential activities that encourage students to examine Israeli life. The text informs students in an honest way that will push them to embrace Israel's unique strengths and qualities, and to confront difficult questions. More than 200 photographs help capture Israel's joys and struggles.

There are nine chapters in *Experience Modern Israel.* The first is an introductory chapter. Each subsequent chapter highlights a major aspect of Israeli history or life.

The text includes these special components designed to enrich the learning experience:

- **Teen Characters** in each chapter help students relate to the material by presenting it through the eyes of a fictional teenager.
- **Online Prompts** direct students to further explore topics using Modern Israel Online, a free downloadable Google Earth file designed to enhance the text. (For more information on this resource, see "Modern Israel Online" [page 7].)
- **"Meet an Israeli"** highlights real Israeli teens who are helping to achieve the country's ideals.
- **"Debate It"** gives students an opportunity to grapple with some of the major conflicts facing Israel's population.
- **"Back to the Sources"** introduces students to Jewish texts that emphasize the ancient Jewish connection to the Land of Israel.
- **"Your Turn"** connects the material to the students' experiences and personalizes Israel in a meaningful way.
- **"Living Jewish Values"** applies Jewish values to modern issues in Israel today and encourages students to consider these values in their own lives.

At the back of the text, you'll also find useful reference material to enhance the learning experience, including:

- **Resources**, a compilation of websites where students can further explore Israel.
- **Say It in Hebrew**, which provides key conversational and travel terms in Hebrew.
- **Glossary** of words introduced in the text. These words are boldfaced on their first reference in the textbook.
- **Index** to help direct teachers and students to information.

Structure of This Lesson Plan Manual

This Lesson Plan Manual serves as a guide for teachers in creating their lessons. The 26 lessons—each approximately 50 minutes long—are complete, comprehensive, and appropriate for teaching *Experience Modern Israel*. In addition, the lessons engage all of the senses through different media, including video, audio, interactive online games and adventures, and online mapping activities.

You may use the lessons exactly as they are, or you can pick and choose components, tailoring the lessons to your needs. You may also want to incorporate some of the assessment activities or projects for further study that are listed at the end of the manual. See below for information about support materials you can use to enrich the lessons. Consider enhancing the technology and Hebrew language components to heighten student engagement and interest. Some suggestions follow in the "Hebrew Connection," "Tech Connection," and "Modern Israel Online" sections of this Introduction.

Lessons for Each Chapter

Each chapter in this manual corresponds to a chapter in the textbook and includes the following elements:

1) An introductory page that contains:

- **Chapter Overview:** A short summary of the chapter's key points
- **Core Concepts:** A listing of the central concepts that students should understand by the chapter's conclusion
- **Learning Objectives:** A list of student objectives
- **Lesson Summaries:** Short overviews of each lesson's central components
- **Hebrew Connection:** A list of Hebrew words highlighted in the chapter
- **Tech Connection:** Useful, creative, and easy ways to utilize technology to enhance student learning

2) Two or three lesson plans that each include:

- **Guiding Question(s):** An overarching question that reflects the main idea of the lesson
- **Materials Needed**: A list of materials
- **Getting Started:** A set induction that introduces students to the material
- **Exploring the Text:** Developmentally appropriate activities, with each component listing the approximate time for its completion
- **Wrapping It Up:** A brief activity or question that encourages reflection on the lesson's essential question

Assessment and Additional Projects

At the end of this Lesson Plan Manual (page 44), you will find suggestions for assessment and additional projects, including interactive online activities, for each chapter. Questions and activities are fact-based and open-ended, to ensure that students are internalizing the material and thinking critically about Israel.

Icons

To help you prepare your lessons, a series of icons identifies certain types of activities. They are:

Mouse: Activities involving Modern Israel Online or other online resources

Hand: Experiential learning activities

Globe: Mapping exercises

House: Activities involving the family or study at home

Printer: Materials that can be printed from www.behrmanhouse.com/EMI

Support Materials

Support content for your lessons is available online at www.behrmanhouse.com/EMI. Worksheets and other supplemental materials are downloadable free at this site. When a lesson refers to something that needs to be printed from this site, a printer icon will appear in the text. You can also download Modern Israel Online from this site. See the "Modern Israel Online" section on page 7 for more information about this interactive online resource.

Hebrew Connection

Study of Israel provides a gateway to modern Hebrew. Hebrew knowledge, at any level, can deepen students' understanding of Israeli culture and our shared history that the language represents. This serves multiple purposes. It will:

- Serve as a springboard for students to continue their study of Hebrew at a more intensive level.
- Strengthen students' ties to the land and its culture.
- Help them learn some key words and phrases that are found in the *t'filot* and *parashot* that they will be studying in preparation for their bat or bar mitzvah.

Each chapter's introductory page lists key words or phrases in Hebrew from the text, with translations. We encourage you to keep a running list of these vocabulary words in your classroom to reinforce the lessons. You can use a large poster board for your Hebrew Connection list, or you could post the words on a class bulletin board.

Tech Connection

Technology is no longer just a component of our students' world. Rather, technology is completely intertwined with their lives. Students have access to technology at home, in school, and increasingly, while on the go. The possibilities for integrating technology into your classroom are infinite and will deepen student engagement and understanding.

The introductory page to each chapter in this Lesson Plan Manual features a "Tech Connection" section with ideas on how to incorporate technology; you'll also find suggestions throughout the lessons. You can adapt these ideas to the technology you have on hand. If your classroom has a SMART Board, or a computer attached to a projector, you can use Internet resources right in class to enrich your lessons. If some of your students have mobile devices with Internet access, like the iPod Touch or the iPad, consider sharing these devices during small group projects. Make sure to approve all sites that you direct students to visit and to supervise students closely when they explore online.

Consider creating an online Wikispace, where your class can share its learning experiences throughout the year. There, teachers and students can post pictures and videos that document student learning, as well as student research. You can also post discussion questions to which students can respond. Detailed instructions on how to launch your class Wikispace can be found at http://help.wikispaces.com/Teacher+Help. Only rudimentary computer knowledge is needed to set up the Wikispace. The instructions at the link above will walk you through the simple setup process. Some prep time is required to use this effectively.

Here are some general suggestions on how to use technology to enrich your lessons:

- Explore and interact with the Modern Israel Online resources for each chapter. (See the "Modern Israel Online" section below for more information.)
- Use a video camera to film your students absorbed in learning experiences, such as giving presentations or engaging in debates; post the videos on the class Wikispace.
- E-mail home or post to your Wikispace questions for parents and students to discuss. Ensure that parents know the Wikispace URL.
- Guide students to two newspaper websites that recount the same story about Israel through two different political viewpoints.
- Download maps of Israel at different times in its history.
- Encourage students to conduct online research about Israel and post their findings on the class Wikispace.
- Utilizing video cameras, have students interview people about their views on Israel, create how-to-videos, film newscasts, and more. Post the videos to your Wikispace.
- Direct students to websites that stream Israeli radio feeds.
- Design an interactive timeline that you can add to as you learn about the formation of the State of Israel.

Modern Israel Online

http://www.behrmanhouse.com/EMI

You'll find references throughout this Lesson Plan Manual to Modern Israel Online, a custom-tailored Google Earth environment with links to further resources, including videos, photos, music, and more. You can download Modern Israel Online at www.behrmanhouse.com/EMI. When a lesson refers to Modern Israel Online, a mouse icon will appear in the text.

Modern Israel Online also lets you explore Israel's geography and landscape. Using this Google Earth environment, students can navigate around the country, zooming in on everything from the salty waters of the Dead Sea to the busy streets of Tel Aviv. They can even create their own virtual tours of Israel, setting "placemarks" on the interactive map and linking related resources.

Here are some suggestions for ways to use Modern Israel Online to enrich your lessons:

- Check out the Modern Israel Online resources for each chapter with your students. Keywords throughout the textbook indicate subjects you can explore further in Modern Israel Online, where dozens of links lead you to videos, virtual tours, music, self-quizzes, and more.
- Provide parents with information on how to access Modern Israel Online and encourage students and parents to explore it together.
- Use Modern Israel Online to explore Israel's geography and to create virtual tours.
- Guide students to create their own placemarks, by locating a place on the Google Earth map and entering their own information or thoughts about that place.
- Use the "Fly to" tab to zoom over the landscape and locate places in Israel. You can also "fly" to your house, your school, or other places that interest you.
- Explore the Layers section in the lower left corner of the screen. You can turn layers on or off to view features such as roads, 3D buildings, the current weather, geographic features, and more.
- Measure distances between two locations by clicking on the Ruler icon at the top of the page.
- Share your placemarks by saving your changes as a new KMZ file and e-mailing it or posting it on your class Wikispace.

Further ideas for using Modern Israel Online can be found in the individual chapters as well as in the "Assessments and Additional Projects" section of this Lesson Plan Manual (page 44). Detailed directions for these and other Google Earth features are easy to find and follow. Click on the "Help" menu at the top of the Google Earth screen and choose "Start-up Tips."

See pages 6–7 of the textbook for an overview on using Modern Israel Online. For additional help and troubleshooting, open the "Modern Israel Online Help" document which you can find on www.behrmanhouse.com/EMI and within the Modern Israel Online application itself.

Teaching Strategies

In addition to the technology ideas noted above, here are some other strategies you may find useful throughout your study of modern Israel.

Opening Rituals

An opening ritual signals that class time has begun and helps set the tone for the lesson. Consider a few options:

1. Open each lesson with a prayer to reinforce the strength of the State of Israel and of the people of Israel:
   Baruch Atah Adonai, Eloheinu Melech ha'olam, oteir Yisrael b'tifarah.
   Blessed are You, Adonai our God, Ruler of the universe, who girds Israel with strength.

2. Post a thought question on the board for students to answer in their notebooks as they arrive. This way, you immediately capture your students' attention. You can develop your own question, use the current lesson's essential question, or use the previous week's as a means for review. Consider playing Israeli music in the background as students write.

3. Show a music video, an Israeli commercial, or a subtitled movie trailer for a current Israeli movie.

Ḥevrutah

Throughout the text, students are asked to work in *ḥevrutah.* Your students may already know that *ḥaver* is Hebrew for "friend." A *ḥevrutah* is a group of two students who work together to study and learn. Each pair studies a shared text and engages in discussion and debate, answering questions and doing projects together. This traditional rabbinic approach to study is used widely in Jewish educational settings.

Notebooks

Consider asking students to keep a notebook or journal throughout the year. Many of the activities in this Lesson Plan Manual require students to think independently or in *ḥevrutah,* and then to write their responses. This allows all students adequate time to consider questions fully before responding aloud. By requiring all students to write an answer, quieter students who may not otherwise respond to a general question will have an answer ready, should you decide to call on them.

Maps

Maps can help students visualize and better understand Israel's geography. Consider hanging a large map of Israel in your classroom to which you can refer when appropriate. It might also be useful to have a world map, so students can see Israel's place in the world, gaining a better understanding of the Diaspora and of Israel's struggles with its neighbors. You'll also find several maps throughout the text, including one in the book's introduction. To bring the map of Israel alive, you can explore Modern Israel Online's interactive map. (For more information on this resource, see "Modern Israel Online" on page 7.)

CHAPTER

1 INTRODUCTION
Visiting Israel

Chapter Overview: This chapter is an introduction to your Israel curriculum. Students follow a fictional peer named Justin as he prepares for his trip to Israel. Like our students, he has some basic knowledge about Israel. He knows that Israel was founded in 1948, that Jewish holidays are national holidays, that Hebrew is spoken on the streets, and that Israel is a country in conflict with its neighbors. He also knows that Israel is the land promised to our ancestors in the Bible. Also, like our students, he has many questions about what Israel is like today.

Core Concepts

- Israel is a thoroughly modern nation with a diverse population and diverse climates.
- Israel is a complex nation, with a unique history, conflicts, people, and culture.
- The word *Yisrael* comes from the biblical story of Jacob wrestling with an angel and can be used to refer to the Jewish people, the modern state of Israel, or the land that has been central to the Jewish people throughout history.

Learning Objectives – Students will:

- Think critically about prior knowledge of Israel and develop questions for future study. (Lesson 1)
- Articulate the origins of the name *Yisrael* as well as explain the difference between *Am Yisrael, Eretz Yisrael*, and *M'dinat Yisrael*. (Lesson 2)

Lesson Summaries

- **Lesson 1:** Through a fun "step-in" activity, students consider their prior knowledge and reflect on what they hope to learn this year.
- **Lesson 2:** Students explore the biblical name *Yisrael*, its history and connection to Jewish concepts, and begin building the class's Hebrew Connection words list.

Hebrew Connection

- **Yisrael**: Name given to Jacob after he wrestles with God. Lit: God wrestler
- **Am Yisrael**: All descendents of Jacob. The Jewish people. Lit: The people of Israel
- **Eretz Yisrael**: The land promised to our ancestors in the Torah. Lit: The Land of Israel
- **M'dinat Yisrael**: The modern state of Israel that was founded in 1948. Lit: The State of Israel
- **Ḥevrutah**: A study partner. The Jewish practice of studying with a partner or *ḥaver*.
- **Kotel**: The remnant of the retaining Western Wall that surrounded the Second Temple in Jerusalem, which was destroyed by the Romans in the year 70 CE.

Tech Connection

- Visit Modern Israel Online with your class and explore the links for this chapter. Take a virtual tour of Israel, see the Kotel Cam, test your knowledge of Israel, and more. See page 7 of this Lesson Plan Manual for more information about Modern Israel Online.
- Direct students to do online research about the Kotel. Then, utilizing Modern Israel Online, create a "placemark" for the Kotel. (Instructions are on www.behrmanhouse.com/EMI.)
- Play classic Israeli songs as students enter the classroom, such as "Bashanah Haba'ah," "Halleluyah," or "Al Kol Eileh."

Chapter 1: Lesson 1

What do students already know about Israel, and what do they want to learn this year?

Materials Needed:
Printout of "Test Your Israel Knowledge" supplement from www.behrmanhouse.com/EMI, index cards, online access

Getting Started: (15 minutes)
Begin with an interactive activity to gauge students' prior knowledge. Direct students to stand in a circle facing one another. Read aloud a series of statements about Israel from the printout "Test Your Israel Knowledge." Students who believe a statement is true, step inside the circle. Students who believe the statement is false, stay still. *(Answers are noted on the page for your reference.)* Consider adding your own statements from the text or from your own knowledge.

Exploring the Text:

1. (5 minutes) Once you have completed the "Getting Started" exercise, ask students: "Did anything surprise you? Did you learn something new about Israel? What questions had agreement? What questions had disagreement? What else do you know about Israel?"

2. (5 minutes) Tell students that you are impressed with what they already know about Israel, but you're sure that they still have many questions. Direct students to locate Justin's questions about Israel on pages 10-13. What questions do they have about Israel? Consider asking students to write their questions on index cards, which you can refer to in planning future lessons.

3. (10 minutes) Visit your school's computer lab to introduce students to Modern Israel Online, which they'll be using throughout the year. Prior to class, download the Google Earth file from www.behrmanhouse.com/EMI. By clicking on the placemarks throughout Modern Israel Online, students can link to information, videos, music, and more about Israel. Encourage students to click on a placemark and see what they find. Ask a few students to share. Explain that they can also zoom in on geographic areas; ask students to find Jerusalem and zoom in on it.

4. (10 minutes) Direct students to look at the **photograph of the Kotel** (page 11). Explain that the Kotel (Western Wall) in Jerusalem is the holiest place for Jews; it is the site where the Temple once stood. After viewing the picture, visit the Kotel Cam on Modern Israel Online to see a live feed of the Kotel. Ask students, "What makes this site holy? What do you think it feels like to stand at the Kotel?" Tell students that no matter where we are, when we pray, we pray in the direction of Jerusalem and the Kotel.

Wrapping It Up: (5 minutes)
Ask students to look at **Israel in Photos** (pages 8–9) and read the captions. Based on what students have learned, encourage them to think about what they would pack for a trip to Israel. Instruct students to complete the section **Your Turn: Packing List** (page 13).

Chapter 1: Lesson 2

Where did Israel's name come from, and what is the difference between *Am Yisrael, Eretz Yisrael,* and *M'dinat Yisrael*?

Materials Needed:

Large piece of butcher paper or poster board, marker, copies of Genesis 32:23-31

Getting Started: (5 minutes)

Write "Israel/*Yisrael*" on the board. Note that *Yisrael* is the Hebrew word for Israel. Ask students to complete **Survey Says** (page 13), and share their results. Discuss how Israel is a modern country with ancient roots. This lesson will focus on Israel's biblical roots and reveal where the name Israel came from.

Exploring the Text:

1. (5 minutes) Introduce the concept of *ḥevrutah* study. Ask if students know the word *ḥaver* (friend), and explain that *ḥevrutah* is the Jewish practice of studying text with a friend. Break students into *ḥevrutah.*

2. (15 minutes) Distribute copies of Genesis 32:23-31, the story of Jacob wrestling the angel. Students work in *ḥevrutah* to read the text, and answer:
   a) Who are the characters in this story?
   b) Who does Jacob think that the man he encountered was?
   c) Why was Jacob's name changed?
   d) What do you think the name *Yisrael* means?
   e) Reconvene as a class to discuss. Explain that *Yisrael* means "He who wrestles with God." Ask: "How do Jews wrestle with God?"

3. (5 minutes) Ask students what the importance of Israel is in the Bible. Direct them to the **Jewish homeland** section (page 10) to find three major links to Israel. (*Israel is the land God promised to our ancestors. It is the land to which Moses led the Jewish people. It is the land where King Solomon built the Holy Temple.*)

4. (5 minutes) Explain that Israel is full of places that have biblical significance. Refer students to **Time Travel** (page 11), and have them help you locate the sites mentioned on a classroom map of Israel.

5. (10 minutes) On the board, write *Am Yisrael, Eretz Yisrael,* and *M'dinat Yisrael* as headings to each of three columns. Explain what they mean. (Refer to the Hebrew Connection on page 5 in this Lesson Plan Manual.) As a class, categorize each of the following terms:
   a) *B'nai Yisrael* (*Am*)
   b) The Kingdom of Israel (*Eretz*)
   c) Knesset (*M'dinat*)
   d) Tel Aviv (*M'dinat*)
   e) Promised Land (*Eretz*)
   f) *Sh'ma Yisrael* (*Am*)
   g) More that you can think of...

Wrapping It Up: (5 minutes)
Start a Hebrew Connection list, a running list of Hebrew vocabulary words that you post in the classroom to reinforce the lessons. You can use butcher paper or a large poster board to keep your list, or you could post the words on a class bulletin board. Based on what they learned in the lesson, ask students to develop definitions for the terms *Am Yisrael, Eretz Yisrael,* and *M'dinat Yisrael* to add to your Hebrew Connection list. Shape student input to ensure that the definitions are correct.

CHAPTER

2 ARTS AND CULTURE
Not Just Fun and Games

Chapter Overview: Israel is a diverse nation with arts, culture, and food representative of Jews who made aliyah from all over the world, as well as of the country's Arab population and other indigenous cultures. Many Israeli restaurants are kosher. Israeli teens play sports, go to the beach, join youth groups, and listen to music that reflects Israel's political and economic climate. The performing arts flourish in Israel, and Israeli studios produce many of the country's television programs and films. Popular radio stations broadcast music by both Israeli and international recording stars.

Core Concepts

- Israelis have a unique culture that has been influenced by the cultures of Jews from around the world who immigrated to Israel, as well as by Arab culture.
- There are many commonalities among American and Israeli teenagers.
- Israel, a small country, produces a disproportionately large amount of art and music.

Learning Objectives – Students will:

- Identify the influences on modern Israeli culture. (Lesson 1)
- Articulate what many Israeli teens do for fun, and compare and contrast that with their own lives by identifying similarities that surprise them and differences that intrigue them. (Lesson 2)
- Locate places online where they can seek out Israeli popular media. (Lesson 3)

Lesson Summaries

- Lesson 1: Students discuss how Israel's immigrants have brought their cultures with them and create an Israeli art gallery.
- Lesson 2: Students create their own *Yom Ha'atzma'ut* poster, make hummus, play an Israeli beach sport, and watch a video about the Israeli Scouts Caravan.
- Lesson 3: Students listen to Israeli music, view Israeli arts, and get a taste of the diversity of arts and culture in Israel.

Hebrew Connection

- **Aliyah**: Immigration to Israel
- **Falafel**: fried balls of ground chickpeas served in a pita filled with sauces, salads, and pickles
- **Kashrut**: Jewish dietary laws
- **Matkot**: Popular Israeli beach sport where players use paddles or racquets to keep a ball in the air without it dropping
- **Olim**: Immigrants to Israel
- **Shawarma**: a pita sandwich made with turkey or lamb
- **Shuk**: market
- **Tzofim**: The Israeli Scouts Federation
- **Yom Ha'atzma'ut**: Israel's Independence Day

Tech Connection

- Visit Modern Israel Online with your class and explore the links for this chapter. Watch a video about the Maccabiah Games, learn to make falafel, listen to some popular Israeli music, and more. See page 7 of this Lesson Plan Manual for more information about Modern Israel Online.
- Direct students to look online for Israeli art, and post the pictures to your class Wikispace.
- Encourage students to watch online music videos from Israeli musicians on YouTube.
- Invite students to upload pictures or videos of Israeli artwork that they have in their homes to your class Wikispace. Ask them to explain the pieces' cultural influences.
- Visit the Bezalel Academy of Arts and Design online at www.bezalel.ac.il/en to view and critique the art portfolios of Israeli students.

Chapter 2: Lesson 1

How does Israel's diverse population influence its arts and culture?

Materials Needed:

Pictures of Israeli art downloaded from Modern Israel Online or other sources*, world map

Getting Started: (10 minutes)

In *ḥevrutah*, students exchange information about their family history, including where their ancestors came from and why they immigrated to America. Consider presenting students with these questions the previous week, so they can discuss them with family members. Reconvene as a class, and ask students to indicate which countries their ancestors came from. Remind students that, like America, Israel has immigrants from the world over.

Exploring the Text:

1. (5 minutes) Ask students which countries they think Israel's *olim* moved from. Make a list of countries, referring students to **National character** (page 14) for help. (*Russia, Poland, Yemen, Iraq, Ethiopia, the United States, and more*) Point out these countries to students on a world map.

2. (5 minutes) Explain that Israel's immigrants have brought their cultures with them and influenced Israeli arts and culture. Students individually read **Visual arts** (page 18) and underline three examples of the contributions of different cultures. *(Eastern European silver Kiddush cups, Yemenite jewelry, Ethiopian embroidery)*

3. (5 minutes) Before class, print out pictures of Israeli artwork along with each artist's biographical information, using Modern Israel Online or other online sources. Paste the biographical information to the back of each picture. Hang the pictures around the classroom, creating an Israeli art gallery. Ask students to look at the pictures and stand by their favorite one. Students discuss what they like about the picture with the other students who chose it.

4. (15 minutes) Explain that cultural influences help shape an artist's style. Cultural influences may include references to the artist's nation of origin, style from that country, depictions of the style of Judaism from that country or region, and so on. Students turn over the artwork to read about the artist. In their notebooks, students write a short art review that answers the following questions:
    a) What did I like about this artwork?
    b) Who is the artist, and where does he or she come from?
    c) How does the artist's country of origin affect the artist's style?
    d) Does this artwork make a statement about Israeli life today, and if so, in what way(s)?

Wrapping It Up: (10 Minutes)
Ask students to share one cultural influence that intrigued them. Finish by explaining that Israeli music, food, fashion, and more are also influenced by the multiple cultures that make up Israeli society.

* Educational Fair Use Guidelines may apply if the teacher chooses the material to print for his or her class only, prints no more than one picture per artist, and properly credits the material.

Chapter 2: Lesson 2

Are Israeli teens like me?

Materials Needed:

Copies of the "My Favorites" worksheet for this lesson printed from www.behrmanhouse.com/EMI and a hummus recipe printed from Modern Israel Online, hummus ingredients, markers, construction paper, bowls, pita bread, plastic spoons, ping-pong paddles, ping-pong balls, TV / DVD player, Israeli Scouts video.

Getting Started: (5 Minutes)

Distribute the worksheet and ask students to indicate their favorite foods, sports, music, and more. Volunteers share what they wrote. Tell students that today we are going to learn a little bit about what Israeli teens like to eat, what sports they play, and what they do for fun.

Exploring the Text:

Students rotate through four different stations for 10 minutes each.

- **Station 1: Bezalel Academy of Arts and Design.** Students imagine that, like Tali, they want to be art students at the Bezalel Academy of Arts and Design. One of their classes is having a competition for the best *Yom Ha'atzma'ut* (Israel Independence Day) poster for this year's national celebration. In small groups, students read **Themes in Israeli art** (page 18) and **Poster art** (page 19), and examine the sample **Independence Day poster** (page 19). Using markers and construction paper, students create their own *Yom Ha'atzma'ut* posters, incorporating images from Israel's religions, history, and culture. Students complete any unfinished posters at home.

- **Station 2: A Taste of Israel.** Students imagine that they are chefs at an Israeli restaurant. Ask them to read **Food favorites** (page 20) and **Recipes from around the world** (page 20), underlining four Middle Eastern items that they would put on their menus and two international dishes. Next, have them make hummus, a Middle Eastern specialty, from the ingredients provided, and sample it with pita bread.

- **Station 3: A Day at the Beach.** Students imagine they are on an Israeli beach. After reading the sections **Popular sports** and **Fun and games at the beach** (page 22), they take the ping-pong balls and paddles and play a modified version of *matkot*, hitting the ball gently within a defined area.

- **Station 4: Israeli Kids.** Students watch a video about the Israeli Scouts Caravan on Modern Israel Online. After viewing the video, they read **Youth groups** (page 23) and complete **Meet an Israeli** (page 23). Ask students what significance the Maccabiah Games have for us in America and for Jews around the world.

Wrapping It Up: (5 minutes)
Students share their reactions to the day with the whole class. How are you like Israeli teens? How are you different?

Chapter 2: Lesson 3

What is unique about Israeli music?

Materials Needed:
Popular Israeli music on a CD or on an MP3 player (choose your favorites, or search for titles mentioned in the textbook such as "The Sticker Song" by Hadag Naḥash, "New Soul" by Yael Naim, or "Bo'ee (Come with Me)" by the Idan Raichel Project), printouts of lyrics, online access

Getting Started: (15 Minutes)
Play two or three popular Israeli songs as students arrive. Once everyone is seated, ask students what they thought of the songs. How does the music sound similar to or different from American music? What new instruments did you hear? Did you like it? What does the music express about Israeli culture? Was there anything unique about this music?

Exploring the Text:

1. (10 minutes) Ask students to read the lyrics to one of the songs you played in class, and talk about how they think the song got its name, and what the lyrics say about Israeli culture. After volunteers offer a few ideas, direct students to the first paragraph under **Popular music** (page 24) to learn about themes in Israeli popular music. Discuss what the diversity of bumper sticker slogans, the subject of "The Sticker Song," says about Israeli culture. (*Israelis have diverse opinions on politics, economics, and religion, and tend to be vocal about expressing them.*) Students can visit the links on Modern Israel Online to hear more popular music.

2. (20 minutes) Visit your school's computer lab. As suggested by the sidebar feature, **Your Turn: Try Something New** (page 27), ask students to circle names of musicians, radio stations, and TV programs cited in the chapter. Next, encourage the class to search online for additional information about each. (Links to many of these resources are available on Modern Israel Online.) Students can read Israeli poetry or view some Israeli art. Students can even watch television clips and movie trailers, or listen to music on YouTube, with supervison.

Wrapping It Up: (5 minutes)
Ask students to share a favorite item they saw, read, or heard from all the artists, musicians, and poets they encountered. Instruct them to indicate a unique characteristic of the art that makes it Israeli. Together, you will get a sense of the diversity of arts and culture in Israel. Discuss how Israeli media is readily accessible in the United States, making it easy for them to continue exploring Israeli culture.

CHAPTER

3 DIVERSE NATION
Israeli Salad

Chapter Overview: Israel is deeply committed to the immigration of Jews from all over the world. Jews seeking a better life, escaping persecution, or desiring to be a part of the Jewish state have made *aliyah* to Israel. Israel is not only home to Jews of varying ethnic and religious identities, but also to non-Jews, including Druze, Christian Arabs, Muslim Arabs, and Bedouins, who together make up Israel's diverse "salad bowl" of identities.

Core Concepts

- Israel is a diverse nation comprised of Jews from all over the world.
- Peoples of many faiths call Israel home.
- The Law of Return guarantees Jews from all over the world the right to Israeli citizenship.

Learning Objectives – Students will:

- Articulate why Israel offers citizenship to all Jews, anywhere and everywhere. (Lesson 1)
- Outline the various communities of Jews who make up the Israeli population, as well as the cultural and religious divisions within the Jewish community. (Lesson 2)
- Explain why many faiths consider Israel to be a holy land, list which groups consider Israel home, and articulate why. (Lesson 3)

Lesson Summaries

- Lesson 1: Students visit their synagogue's sanctuary to learn about the word *aliyah* and then learn about Israel's Law of Return.
- Lesson 2: Students take on the roles of people from Israel's different immigrant communities and give presentations telling the story of each group.
- Lesson 3: Students explore non-Jewish religious communities in Israel and examine some of the struggles of co-existing in such close proximity.

Hebrew Connection

- **Kibbutz Galuyot**: Ingathering of exiles
- **Sabra**: a Jew born in Israel. It also refers to the fruit of a cactus, which is prickly on the outside and sweet on the inside
- **Ulpan**: Intensive Hebrew immersion class

Tech Connection

- Visit Modern Israel Online with your class and explore the links for this chapter. See a video about Yemenite Jewish culture, tour Christian and Muslim holy sites in Israel, delve deeper into the history of various groups that have made *aliyah*, and more. See page 7 of this Lesson Plan Manual for more information about Modern Israel Online.
- Videotape your student presentations from Lesson 2, and post them to your class Wikispace.
- In Lesson 3, go to the school computer lab and visit the Israeli Embassy's kids site to learn about Israel's religious diversity.
- Visit Israel's Ministry of Foreign Affairs Web site (www.mfa.gov.il) to learn about the *aliyah* process and about the Law of Return.
- If you know an Israeli who has made *aliyah*, arrange for the class to interview him or her via webcam.

Chapter 3: Lesson 1

What is aliyah to Israel, and how does the Law of Return enable Jews from all over the world to become Israeli citizens?

Materials Needed:
Access to your synagogue's sanctuary; optional: *siddur, Tanach*, a copy of Israel's Declaration of Independence

Getting Started: (15 minutes)
Visit your synagogue's sanctuary to discuss the word *aliyah*. With the help of your rabbi, cantor, or education director, remove the Torah from the ark, undress it, and place it on a lectern that students gather around. Have students share what they know about being called to the Torah for an *aliyah*. Discuss how *aliyah* literally means "going up" and that being called "up" to the Torah is a spiritually elevating event. Ask: "Have you ever heard of anyone making *aliyah* to Israel? What does that mean?" Explain that when Jews immigrate to Israel, it is called making *aliyah*, because moving to the Jewish holy land is also a spiritual elevation. Return to the classroom.

Exploring the Text:

1. (10 minutes) With their *ḥevrutah* partner, students read **Jewish diversity** (page 28) and underline each of the different groups of Jews mentioned. Discuss as a class, recording the answers on the board. Partners then answer the questions in **Israeli Salad** (page 29) and share their ideas with the class.

2. (3 Minutes) Discuss how Jews from around the world, representing a variety of religious observances, have made *aliyah*. Since 1950, any Jew can immigrate to Israel under the Law of Return.

3. (12 Minutes) Examine three sources that describe the importance of Jewish immigration to Israel, one from the *Tanach*, one from prayer, and one from Israel's Declaration of Independence. Three volunteers each read aloud one of the quotes listed in **Living Jewish Values** (page 31). (If time permits, students can read the excerpts directly from the sources: the *Tanach*, a *siddur*, and the Declaration of Independence.)

4. (5 minutes) With their *ḥevrutah* partners, students read the next paragraph of "Living Jewish Values," starting **"The prophet Isaiah promised it…"** (page 31). Ask: "Why is Israel's commitment to Jewish immigration important to the Jewish people? Why did Israel enact the Law of Return? (*Possible answers include: to ensure that Jews have a safe place to go in case of anti-Semitism or persecution.*)

Wrapping It Up: (5 Minutes)
Ask students who have relatives in Israel or who know someone who has made *aliyah* to share their stories. As a backup, be prepared to share the experiences of a congregant, former student, friend, or relative who has made *aliyah*.

Chapter 3: Lesson 2

Who are the Jews who make up Israel's population?

Materials Needed:

Carrot sticks, Sabra brand hummus, costumes representative of different *olim* (optional), video camera (optional)

Getting Started: (5 minutes)

Distribute carrot sticks and Sabra brand hummus. While students are noshing, remind them that hummus is a food staple in Israel and is becoming more popular in the United States.

Exploring the Text:

1. (5 minutes) Tell students that "sabra," in addition to being the name of a brand of hummus, is the Hebrew word for Jews born in Israel. A volunteer reads the caption for the **cactus photo** (page 28). Ask: "Why might native-born Israelis be called sabras?" (*Because like the cactus, they are considered prickly on the outside and sweet on the inside.*) Remind students that while some Israelis are sabras, others are *olim* (immigrants).

2. (20 minutes) Break the class into four groups. Assign each a prominent Jewish immigrant group: Yemenite Israelis, Russian Israelis, Ethiopian Israelis, and Anglo Israelis. Point out the countries of origin on a world map. Each group prepares a 3-minute presentation about its assigned immigrant population, referring to the appropriate text: **Yemenite Jews** (page 30), **Russian Jews** (page 31), **Ethiopian Jews** (page 32), or **Anglo Jews** (page 33). Encourage students to present the information in a creative format, such as acting out the experience of a fictional character from the immigrant group. Consider providing some simple costumes (like an American baseball cap and an Ethiopian-style *kippah*). Students should consider these questions:
    a) How did I or my family get to Israel and why?
    b) When did my family move to Israel?
    c) What do I look like and how do I traditionally dress?
    d) What challenges has my family faced in adjusting to Israeli society?
    e) What contributions have my people made to Israeli society?

3. (12 Minutes) Students present their reports to their classmates. Optional: Film the presentations and post them to your class Wikispace.

Wrapping It Up: (8 Minutes)
A volunteer reads aloud the Hebrew text and its translation in **Back to the Sources** (page 33). Students individually answer the question below: "How is the State of Israel like a family?" Discuss their responses. Lastly, as a class, sing the verse, *"Hinei Mah-Tov."*

Chapter 3: Lesson 3

What faiths other than Judaism call Israel home, and why? How do Israelis from different religions get along?

Materials Needed:
Online access

Getting Started: (5 minutes)
Remind students that non-Jews are also part of Israel's population. Ask students to guess what percentage of Israelis are not Jewish. (*nearly 25%*) Each student guesses, and whoever comes the closest without going over wins a small prize, like an Israeli chocolate bar.

Exploring the Text:

1. (10 minutes) Ask: "What ethnic groups and religions call Israel home, and why?" Direct students to scan pages 34-35 for answers. Give them a few minutes to write, and then ask them to share their responses. Answers include: Christians, Christian Arabs, Muslim Arabs, Baha'i, Druze, and Bedouins. Identify any groups students did not mention.

2. (20 minutes) Visit the school's computer lab. Direct students to the "Kids" section of the Israeli Embassy website (www.israelemb.org/kids), which you can also access from Modern Israel Online. Ask students to visit the Jerusalem section of the "Tour Israel" link. There, students can study the Temple Mount, the Church of the Holy Sepulchre, as well as the Western Wall. Ask students to record three facts about each of those sites. (Information about the Temple Mount and the Church of the Holy Sepulchre also appears in **A holy land** and in photo captions on page 34. Information about the Western Wall is in the caption on page 11.) Ask: "What do these sites have in common? How are they different? Which would you like to visit? Why?"

3. (10 Minutes) Discuss how Israel's diverse population generally gets along, but that sometimes tensions rise among different religious groups. Direct students to **Getting along** (page 36) and **Separate worlds** (page 37) to discover some of the conflicts facing Israelis today. Invite students to think of a potential solution for one of these conflicts, and then share it with the class.

Wrapping It Up: (10 Minutes)
In *ḥevrutah,* students compile a list of the various populations in Israel. They may list different faiths, Jews from different countries, Jews with different skin colors, Jews with different levels of religious observances, and more. Make a list on the board to serve as a chapter summary.

CHAPTER

4 A JEWISH STATE
There's No Place Like Home

Chapter Overview: Israel is a Jewish state, which is reflected in every aspect of daily life. Judaism is everywhere—not just in the synagogue, but on the street, in school, and on TV. Despite being a Jewish state, Israel is a representative democracy with a government that is inclusive of other religious and ethnic groups. Israel faces unique internal struggles about the role of religion in the daily lives of Israelis.

Core Concepts

- Israel does not have "separation of church and state" as we do in the United States and Canada.
- The Knesset's parliamentary structure requires parties to work cooperatively to forge a coalition.
- Israelis often disagree about the role of religion in their daily lives and how that should manifest itself on a state level.
- Hebrew and Arabic are both official languages of Israel.

Learning Objectives – Students will:

- Discuss the intricacies of the Israeli parliamentary system and the difficulties of creating a strong coalition government. (Lesson 1)
- Demonstrate knowledge of the complexity of some of the current internal conflicts among Israel's Jewish population. (Lesson 2)
- Propose some ideas for cooperation among secular and religious Israelis, as well as appreciate the religious diversity in Israel. (Lesson 3)

Lesson Summaries

- Lesson 1: Students learn about the complexity of the Israeli government by creating their own coalition governments using an ice-cream sundae as a metaphor.
- Lesson 2: Students debate various topics of importance to Jews in Israel relating to the role of religion in daily life.
- Lesson 3: By creating multilingual signs for classroom items, students see Israel as a home for more than just Jews.

Hebrew Connection

- **Beit Din**: Court of justice
- **Halachah**: Jewish religious law
- **Hatikvah**: Israel's national anthem. Lit: The hope
- **Knesset**: Israeli Parliament
- **Yeshivot**: Institutions for advanced Jewish learning

Tech Connection

- Visit Modern Israel Online with your class and explore the links for this chapter. Watch a video of Jews all over the world singing "Hatikvah," play a game to learn about the Knesset, study the full text of the Law of Return, and more. See page 7 of this Lesson Plan Manual for more information about Modern Israel Online.
- Watch various performances of "Hatikvah" online.
- Post the debate questions from Lesson 2 to the discussion board on your Wikispace page. Encourage families to discuss them at home.
- Hold a competition in which students make door signs reminiscent of Israeli street signs for their rooms at home using digital art software. Invite students to upload them to the class Wikispace.

Chapter 4: Lesson 1

How is Israel's government structured?

Materials Needed:
Ice cream, safety pins, printouts of government comparison worksheets and ice-cream sundae topping pages from www.behrmanhouse.com/EMI, access to the music for "Hatikvah" and "The Moldau" by Bedrich Smetana

Getting Started: (5 minutes)
Play an excerpt from Bedrich Smetana's "The Moldau." Ask students if they recognize the melody. (*"Hatikvah," Israel's national anthem)* Explain that both "Hatikvah," and the "The Moldau" are based on the same Eastern European folksong. The Moldau is a river in Eastern Europe.

Exploring the Text:

1. (5 minutes) While listening to "Hatikvah," students silently read the translation of the lyrics (page 39). A volunteer reads aloud the second paragraph in **Something to sing about** (page 39). Ask students the questions at the bottom: "Does "Hatikvah" speak to all Israelis? . . . " Remind students that "Hatikvah" has Eastern European origins and refers to Zion toward the East. Use a world map to illustrate this. Discuss how Israelis come from many viewpoints and that representatives from all viewpoints can have a say in Israel's government.

2. (5 minutes) In *ḥevrutah,* students read **Religion and government** (page 38) and compare the U.S. philosophy of "separation of church and state" to Israel's policy. Ask partners to list five examples of how Israel is a Jewish state, referring to the text.

3. (10 Minutes) Using the government comparison worksheets, students compare and contrast the U.S. and Israeli governments or the Canadian and Israeli governments, referring to **Israeli government 101** (page 40) and **The Knesset** and **Building a coalition** (page 41). *(Both United States and Canada versions of the comparison worksheets are provided, and a teacher edition is provided as well, with the information for Israel's government filled in.)*

4. (15 Minutes) Build a "coalition" ice-cream sundae to demonstrate how the Knesset works. Assign each student a sundae component. The two largest parties, Kadima and Likud, are represented by chocolate and vanilla ice cream. They serve as the foundations for the pending coalitions (ice-cream sundaes). The sundae toppings are the other parties. Each topping has preferences as to which flavor it wants to be with or which topping it doesn't want to be with. Distribute the signs and rules for each topping, which you printed from www.behrmanhouse.com/EMI. Students fold the signs on the dotted lines (so that each student only knows his or her own sundae component's rules), and affix them with safety pins to their shirts. Students negotiate which flavor to join, and the flavors work to gain a majority. For example, if Oreos want to be with vanilla, but not with whipped cream, they may tell vanilla that they will not join unless vanilla kicks out whipped cream.

Wrapping It Up: (10 Minutes)
Distribute ice cream, and discuss the activity. Did students build a coalition? What obstacles did they overcome? Did they make any concessions? Discuss how in the Knesset, each party must make sacrifices. Explain that the Knesset's coalitions are often fragile. If one party is upset by the leadership's actions, it can leave the coalition, destabilizing the government and necessitating a new election.

Chapter 4: Lesson 2

What are some internal conflicts among Israel's Jewish population?

Materials Needed:
Timer

Getting Started: (5 minutes)
Ask students what Israel's Law of Return states. They may recall this from Lesson 3.1; if not, refer them to **The Law of Return** (page 42). Note that the Law of Return, which offers Israeli citizenship to all Jews, raises the question of "Who is a Jew?" Israel's diverse Jewish population has divergent views on this and many other topics.

Exploring the Text:

1. (5 minutes) Tell students that today they'll debate some of Israel's hot-button issues. Three volunteers serve as the *Beit din* (court) and decide the winning team for each debate. Divide the rest of the students into two teams.

   Explain the rules: There will be three debates. Teams have 5 minutes to prepare for each debate, and then 5 minutes to debate. Teams make an opening statement and take turns making their arguments. The team that wins two out of three debates wins. The *Beit din* judges teams on the cohesion of their arguments, how well teammates work together to present their arguments, and their behavior toward the opposing team. During each 5-minute preparation period, the *Beit din* should review the material so they can be prepared to spot inconsistencies in the teams' arguments.

2. (30 Minutes) Debate it!

   Topic #1: The Law of Return properly represents "who is a Jew." (Refer students to **"Who is a Jew?"** [page 43].)
   Team 1: Agrees
   Team 2: Disagrees

   Topic #2: Israel's Orthodox citizens should be required to serve in the military like everybody else. (Refer students to **Army service** [pages 44-45].)
   Team 1: Agrees
   Team 2: Disagrees

   Topic #3: Public buses should run on Shabbat in Israel. (Refer students to **Debate It** [page 45].)
   Team 1: Agrees
   Team 2: Disagrees

Wrapping It Up: (10 Minutes)
The *Beit din* declares a winner based on the above criteria. Ask students how they really feel about these issues. Did any of their opinions change as a result of the debates? What are some of the benefits and drawbacks of not having a "separation of church and state" in Israel? What was it like for students who debated an issue from the side they disagreed with?

Chapter 4: Lesson 3

How does Israel's religious and cultural diversity manifest itself in the day-to-day life of Israelis?

Materials Needed:

Construction paper, markers, online access

Getting Started: (5 minutes)

Ask: "What language or languages would you expect to find on Israeli street signs?" Prompt students by asking them to think about what groups of people call Israel home. Once you have gathered their thoughts, explain that Israeli street signs are in three languages: Hebrew, Arabic, and English.

Exploring the Text:

1. (5 minutes) Discuss whether students feel that the Israeli signs should be in three languages. Why or why not? (*Possible answers might include: The signs should only be in Hebrew because Israel is a Jewish state; the signs should be in all three languages because Israel is home to people who speak each of these languages.*)

2. (15 minutes) Direct students to the **photo of the street sign** (page 46) to illustrate what Israeli street signs look like. Students will make their own tri-lingual signs for the classroom. Using "Google translate" (http://translate.google.com), they find Hebrew and Arabic translations for classroom items, such as window, desk, chair, etc. Distribute construction paper and markers, and encourage students to decorate the signs.

3. (10 minutes) Ask students to identify other ways that Israel recognizes its diversity, referring them to **Two official languages** and **National holidays** (page 46). (*Israeli law states that Arab citizens have a right to receive information they can understand, so TV shows, medicine labels, and election information are translated into Arabic. Schools and businesses have optional holiday schedules, depending on whether they celebrate Jewish or Muslim holidays.*) Ask students whether they agree or disagree with these policies. Point out that while Israel is a Jewish state, it supports freedom of religion.

4. (10 Minutes) Remind students that Israeli Jews are also diverse. Students read **Meet an Israeli** (page 47). Discuss why it may be difficult for secular and religious Israelis to get along. Guide students in developing answers based on the chapter's information, including the Lesson 2 debates. Instruct students to think like Ortal, and propose some methods to promote understanding among secular and religious Israelis.

Wrapping It Up: (10 minutes)

In *ḥevrutah,* students identify groups in the United States and Canada who could use increased understanding for each other. *(political parties, different races, different socio-economic groups, Jews and Muslims, etc.)* Students brainstorm ways to improve communication among these groups and consider how increased communication can build understanding and respect.

CHAPTER

5 LAYERS OF HISTORY
War and Peace

Chapter Overview: Israel is layered with history. Jewish history is in the museums, in the streets, and buried underground, waiting to be uncovered by archaeologists. Throughout history, Israel has been home to Jews as well as many other civilizations. After the Second Temple was destroyed, Jews dispersed to the Diaspora. Jewish immigration to modern Israel occurred in major waves. Spurred by the injustices of 1895's Dreyfus Affair, Theodor Herzl led a campaign to establish a permanent homeland for the Jewish people in the Land of Israel. In 1948, the State of Israel was established. Israel has fought many wars to ensure its survival and continues to struggle to create a lasting peace.

Core Concepts

- Since the Second Temple in Jerusalem was destroyed in 70 CE, Jews primarily have lived in the Diaspora, though some Jews immigrated to the Land of Israel.
- A series of historical events led to Israel's formation as a state.
- Israel fought to become a state and continues to struggle to maintain its existence.
- Israel has come close to negotiating a lasting peace with the Palestinians but has yet to achieve that ideal.

Learning Objectives – Students will:

- Explain why Jews moved to the Diaspora in 70 CE, as well as the key events and figures that led to Israel's formation in 1948. (Lesson 1)
- Discuss Israel's major military conflicts and explain the events that led to each conflict. (Lesson 2)
- Articulate a basic understanding of Israel's current conflicts with the Palestinians and with surrounding nations. (Lesson 3)

Lesson Summaries

- Lesson 1: Students create an interactive online timeline for the events that led to Israel's establishment.
- Lesson 2: Students continue their timelines, creating entries for Israel's major military conflicts.
- Lesson 3: Students review Israel's history and discuss the root causes of conflict with the Palestinians.

Hebrew Connection

- **Haganah:** A militia created in the 1920s to protect Jewish settlers in Palestine, precursor to the Israel Defense Forces

Tech Connection

- Visit Modern Israel Online with your class and explore the links for this chapter. Discover archaeological treasures, play an interactive game about Israel's history from ancient times to the modern, and view a clip of David Ben-Gurion reading Israel's Declaration of Independence. See page 7 of this Lesson Plan Manual for more information about Modern Israel Online.
- Use publishing software to create newspaper pages, complete with headlines and stories, for significant dates in Israel's history.
- Visit http://theicenter.org/educatorresource/toldot-yisrael to watch videos of people recalling their memories about the establishment of Israel in 1948. Encourage students to interview older relatives about what they remember about the establishment of Israel, film it, and post it to your class Wikispace.

Chapter 5: Lesson 1

What events led to Israel's establishment in 1948?

Materials Needed:

The supplement "Digital Timeline Instructions" from www.behrmanhouse.com/EMI (you can use this to set up the framework for your timeline before class), online access.

Getting Started: (5 minutes)

Before students arrive in class, write on the board, "What does it mean for a place to have 'layers of history'?" In *ḥevrutah*, ask students to propose possible answers. Discuss how Israel has been controlled by many different civilizations since the Second Temple was destroyed in the year 70 CE and Jews were forced to move to the Diaspora. Thus, Israel has multiple layers of history, spanning time, culture, and religion.

Exploring the Text:

1. (5 minutes) Students thumb through **pages 48-51** and **page 54** to find out who controlled the Land of Israel during different time periods. (*Assyrians, Babylonians, Persians, Greeks, Romans, Ottomans, the British*) Most of the answers are in **Many civilizations** (page 49). Note that from biblical times until 70 CE, Jews mostly controlled the land.

2. (5 minutes) Explain that since 70 CE, Jews have lived in the Diaspora (outside of Israel). Use a classroom map, or refer students to the **map** on page 51, to locate Diaspora communities. (*Troyes, Hamburg, Vienna, Vilna, Cordoba, Aleppo, Baghdad, etc.*) Note that between the years 70 and 1948, neither Jews nor Palestinian Arabs had sovereign control over the Land of Israel.

3. (5 minutes) Make a list on the board of historical events that led to Israel's establishment in 1948:
   - 1882—First Aliyah
   - 1895—Dreyfus Affair
   - 1897—First Zionist Congress
   - 1904—Second Aliyah
   - 1917—Balfour Declaration
   - 1920—Haganah Formed
   - 1945—WWII Ends/Displaced Persons
   - 1947—UN Partition Plan

   Tell students that the class will be making a timeline about Israel's history. Working individually or in small groups—depending on your class size—students will become experts on one of the listed events. They will create a one- or two-paragraph summary for a timeline entry either online or by making a poster. Students can embed related pictures, videos, and music in digital timelines.

4. (30 Minutes) Using the textbook (pages 50-56) and Modern Israel Online sources, students research their assigned historical event and develop timeline entries. To understand their event's context, students explore support information for the events before and after theirs. Consider having students find additional resources online; be sure to monitor Internet use. For help, review the detailed instructions for creating an interactive digital timeline at www.behrmanhouse.com/EMI. If you prefer, students can create the timeline by hand or with computer printouts, designing small posters for each event to display in the classroom.

Wrapping It Up: (5 Minutes) If students need more time for the project, assign it to them to complete at home. Provide them with the log-in information for the digital timeline, and consider e-mailing instructions home to parents.

Chapter 5: Lesson 2

What wars has Israel fought throughout its history?

Materials Needed:
Recording of "Hatikvah," downloaded from Modern Israel Online, CD or MP3 player, online access

Getting Started: (10 minutes)
A volunteer, acting as David Ben-Gurion on the day that Israel declared its independence, reads an excerpt from Israel's Declaration of Independence (**caption**, page 57). Consider playing "Hatikvah" and asking students to stand and join in singing, as the crowd did on May 14, 1948, after Ben-Gurion read the Declaration of Independence. Direct students to the **translation of "Hatikvah"** (page 39). Reflect as a group on what it must have felt like for the Jewish people in Israel in 1948 after almost 2,000 years of exile from their homeland.

Exploring the Text:

1. (5 minutes) Tell students that this week, they will learn about Israel's War of Independence and the subsequent wars that Israel fought against its neighbors to maintain its independence. First, answer any technical questions students may have about last week's timeline project.

2. (5 Minutes) Prepare students to continue their timeline (begun in Chapter 5: Lesson 1), focusing on military conflicts and related issues since 1948. Write these events on the board:
   - 1948—Declaring Independence
   - 1948—War of Independence
   - 1948—Palestinian Arab Refugees
   - 1948–1952—Israel's Jewish Population Explosion
   - 1967—Six-Day War
   - 1973—Yom Kippur War
   - 1979—Israel and Egypt Sign Peace Treaty

   Like last week, students will work individually or in small groups—depending on your class size—and become experts on one of the listed events. They will create a one- or two-paragraph summary for a timeline entry either online or by making a poster. Students can embed related pictures, videos, and music in digital timelines.

3. (20 minutes) Instruct students to bring their textbooks to the computer lab. Using the textbook (pages 57-61) and Modern Israel Online sources, students research their assigned historical event and develop timeline entries. To understand their event's context, students explore support information for the events before and after theirs. Consider having students find additional resources online; be sure to monitor Internet use. Detailed instructions for creating an interactive digital timeline are at www.behrmanhouse.com/EMI. If students need more time for the project, assign it as homework or eliminate the "Wrapping It Up" activity.

Wrapping It Up: (10 Minutes)
Given all of the conflict in the Middle East, encourage students to consider whether things could have played out differently if a Jewish state had been founded elsewhere. Students read **Debate It** (page 53) and discuss the Uganda Plan. Ask whether in retrospect they think Herzl was correct to forgo a Jewish homeland in Uganda and work toward one in the Land of Israel.

Chapter 5: Lesson 3

How did the events in Israel's history contribute to the current conflict between the Israelis and Palestinians?

Materials Needed:
Online access

Getting Started: (10 minutes)
Share the famous George Santayana quote: "Those who cannot remember the past are condemned to repeat it." Explain that this piece of wisdom was made famous in reference to the Holocaust but that it holds true in other contexts as well. Ask students to share why this is true and how it might be related to the conflict between Israelis and Palestinians.

Exploring the Text:

1. (30 Minutes). Students explore the timeline they've created. Using the 10 items below, give students 1 minute to explore each topic, and then take 2 minutes to ask them the three questions below. If this activity takes longer than 30 minutes, consider focusing on the events that you would like to stress most, or skip the "Wrapping It Up" activity.
   - 1897—First Zionist Congress
   - 1917—Balfour Declaration
   - 1945—WWII Ends/Displaced Persons
   - 1947—UN Partition Plan
   - 1948—Declaring Independence
   - 1948—War of Independence
   - 1948—Palestinian Arab Refugees
   - 1967—Six-Day War
   - 1973—Yom Kippur War
   - 1979—Israel and Egypt sign peace treaty

   Questions:
   a) What is the timeline item about?
   b) How does it relate to the previous item?
   c) How does it contribute to the current conflict?

2. (10 minutes) Explain that despite this difficult history, Israel has at times come close to negotiating a lasting peace with Palestinians. In *ḥevrutah*, students read **Continuing conflict** (page 62) through **Continued efforts** (page 63) to learn about the current conflict. Ask each *ḥevrutah* to share one item they learned about the peace process. Then, ask one student to read aloud the section **The future** (page 63). Ask students: "Have you heard anything in the news recently pertaining to Israeli security?" If yes, discuss it. If not, be prepared to bring up a recent issue.

Wrapping It Up: (5 Minutes)
Complete **Back to the Sources** (page 63) as a group, brainstorming ways to work toward a lasting peace. Discuss how achieving peace in the Middle East is exceptionally complex and that we have only begun to scratch the surface of the issue. Encourage students to be a part of the peace process by writing letters to their local representatives and Israel's prime minister.

CHAPTER

6 SECURITY AND CONFLICT
In the Headlines

Chapter Overview: The Israel Defense Forces (IDF) serve a vital role in Israel's safety and security. Service is compulsory, with some exceptions. Men must serve for three years and women for two years. There are various branches of the military, each with unique functions. Conflicts exist between Israelis and Palestinians, and there is much controversy about how best to achieve peace. Progress toward peace has been successful at times, but there have also been many setbacks.

Core Concepts

- Israel has a strong military with compulsory service.
- Peace is difficult to achieve, but Israel is committed to working toward it, despite many setbacks.
- Each student can help make a difference in working toward peace.

Learning Objectives – Students will:

- Articulate what the IDF is, what its values are, what its different branches are, who serves, and why. (Lesson 1)
- Discuss the complexities of Israel's struggle for security amid hostility. (Lesson 2)
- Consider their role as Americans/Canadians in promoting peace between Israel and its neighbors, as well as identify some of the historical landmarks and pitfalls of the peace process. (Lesson 3)

Lesson Summaries

- Lesson 1: Students report on the roles of different IDF branches and create a flyer encouraging those exempt from the army to sign up for Sherut Leumi (National Service).
- Lesson 2: Students debate issues surrounding Israel's struggle for security.
- Lesson 3: Students learn about various organizations working toward peace in Israel and the U.S. government's role in the peace process.

Hebrew Connection

- **Pidyon sh'vuyim**: redeeming captives
- **Sherut Leumi**: national service
- **Tzahal**: Israel Defense Forces

Tech Connection

- Visit Modern Israel Online with your class and explore the links for this chapter. View photos from the Israeli Air Force, watch a video about the security fence, learn about an organization that promotes understanding between Jewish and Arab teens, and more. See page 7 of this Lesson Plan Manual for more information about Modern Israel Online.
- Visit the website of A Package from Home (www.apackagefromhome.org), an organization that sends care packages to Israeli soldiers. Check out the "Honor Roll" link for information on how your students can send letters of support and encouragement to be included in these care packages.
- Using Modern Israel Online, visit the websites of the organizations discussed in **Creative dialogue** (page 75) to learn about creative ways Israeli youth are working toward peace, and consider involvement as part of bar/bat mitzvah projects.

Chapter 6: Lesson 1

What is the Israel Defense Forces (IDF)? Who serves in the IDF and why or why not? What are the branches and what are their functions?

Materials Needed:
Markers, construction paper

Getting Started: (5 minutes)
Ask: "What would you like to do after you graduate high school?" Elicit student responses, which may include college, working, the military, etc. Once you gather the responses on the board, explain that most Israeli teens do not get to make that decision, because service is compulsory in the IDF (*Tzahal*). Young men serve for a minimum of three years and young women for a minimum of two.

Exploring the Text:

1. (10 Minutes) Students individually read **Society and the army** (page 65). Ask: "Who serves in the army?" (*men and women, rich and poor, immigrants and sabras, Israelis from all walks of life*) List the answers on the board. Ask: "Who is exempt from serving in the IDF?" Refer students to the first two paragraphs of **Alternatives to the Army** (page 65). (*religiously observant women, Arab Israelis, yeshiva students, people with disabilities*) List on the board. Ask students why each group may be exempt.

2. (10 Minutes) As directed in **Alternatives to the Army** (page 65), students create a flyer encouraging those exempt from the army to sign up for *Sherut Leumi* (National Service). Students present their flyers to the class.

3. (15 minutes) Divide students into four groups. Assign each a military branch featured in the text: Armored Corps (**Border security**, page 66), the Military Police Corps (**Checkpoints,** page 67), Air Force (**Airport safety**, page 70), and Aman (**Intelligence**, page 71). Each group writes a one-to-two sentence overview of the branch's role and presents it to the class. Ask: "Which branch of the army would you want to serve in? Why? Which branch do you think is most critical to Israel's security? Why?"

Wrapping It Up: (10 Minutes)
Students stand and together read aloud the **IDF's oath of allegiance** (page 64), as if they were 18-year-olds being inducted into the IDF. Then ask: "How would America/Canada be different if we had compulsory military service? Would your life be any different? Would it be better? Worse?" Discuss as a class.

Note: Consider condensing this lesson and inviting a former Israeli soldier to class to speak about his or her experience in the army.

Chapter 6: Lesson 2

What are some of the ethical struggles that Israel faces in its dealings with Palestinians?

Materials Needed:
Timer

Getting Started: (5 minutes)
On the board, write: "Why is it important for Israel to have strong security?" Students offer responses. Discuss how security is essential in Israel because the country is surrounded by hostile neighbors, some of whom do not recognize Israel's right to exist.

Exploring the Text:

1. (5 minutes) Tell students that today, like they did a number of weeks ago, they'll debate some of Israel's hot-button issues. This time, the issues are security related. Remind students that Israel must balance its security needs with humanitarian concerns—as emphasized in **Military ethics** (page 72). Three volunteers serve as the *Beit din* (court) and decide the winning team for each debate. Divide the rest of the students into two teams.

   Explain the rules: There will be three debates. Teams have 5 minutes to prepare for each debate,and then 5 minutes to debate. Teams make an opening statement and take turns making their arguments. The team that wins two out of three debates wins. The *Beit din* judges teams on the cohesion of their arguments, how well teammates work together to present their arguments, and their behavior toward the opposing team. During each 5-minute preparation period, the *Beit din* should review the material so they can find inconsistencies in the teams' arguments.

2. (30 Minutes) Debate it!

   Topic #1: Building the security fence in its current location was a smart and acceptable policy. (Refer students to **Security fence** [page 67].)
   Team 1: Agrees
   Team 2: Disagrees

   Topic #2: Checkpoints placed throughout the territories to prevent terrorist attacks are essential, even though they infringe on the privacy of Palestinians. (Refer students to **Checkpoints** [page 67].)
   Team 1: Agrees
   Team 2: Disagrees

   Topic #3: There are times when the price is too steep for *pidyon sh'vuyim* (redeeming captives). (Refer students to **Living Jewish Values** [page 72].)
   Team 1: Agrees
   Team 2: Disagrees

Wrapping It Up: (10 Minutes)
The *Beit din* declares a winner based on the above criteria. Ask students how they really feel about these issues. Did any of their opinions change as a result of the debates? What was it like for those students who debated an issue from the side they disagreed with? Would their opinions change if they were Palestinians living in the territories? What about if they were Israeli Jews?

Chapter 6: Lesson 3

What progress has been made toward peace between Israel and the Palestinians? What have been some of the pitfalls in the peace process?

Materials Needed:

Computer or DVD player and TV to watch downloaded video

Getting Started: (5 minutes)

On the board, write: "Why is peace in Israel important to the international community? To the United States?" Discuss as a class. (*Possible answers include: because the region has been in conflict for so long, the international community cares about it deeply, many influential Americans have ties to Israel, Israel is the home to many of the world's religions, Israel is the only democracy in the Middle East.*) Use a world map to point out Israel's strategic location.

Exploring the Text:

1. (15 minutes) Students individually read **Debate It** (page 71). Ask students to move to one side of the room if they identify with the "hawk" and the other if they identify with the "dove." Then, direct students to do the same thing with "land for peace," moving to one side of the room if they support it, the other side if they do not. Each time, have volunteers share why they chose their position and discuss the pros and cons of each approach.

2. (10 minutes) Students individually read about Seeds of Peace in **Creative Dialogue** (page 75) and then watch a brief movie about the organization, following the link on Modern Israel Online.

3. (10 minutes) Direct students to read all of **Creative Dialogue** (page 75) and circle the words that tell who the program is aimed at, what the goal of the program is, and how it is achieved. Ask the questions at the bottom of the sidebar: "What do each of these programs have in common? Why do you think the programs are targeted at kids?" (*Possible answers include: because children are the future leaders, children usually don't have the biases that adults may have.*)

4. (5 minutes) Remind students that American presidents have moderated many of the peace negotiations between Israel and neighboring countries, referring them to the **photo with President Bill Clinton** (page 74). Ask students to consider how the United States can continue to influence the peace process.

Wrapping It Up: (5 minutes)

Facilitate a discussion about the importance of peace in Israel for Jews around the world. Ask: "Why is it important to us even though we don't live there?" End by asking students how they can help promote peace. (*Answers might include: volunteering with an organization that promotes peace, being an advocate for peace in discussions with peers and adults, teaching their younger siblings about Israel, completing a bar/bat mitzvah project in which they raise funds for an organization that promotes peace.*)

CHAPTER

7 THE ENVIRONMENT
The Great Outdoors

Chapter Overview: Israel is only the size of New Jersey, yet its climate and terrain are vastly varied, providing a wide array of beautiful landscapes and natural resources. Like other developed nations, Israel faces serious environmental problems. In recent years, Israel has made significant strides in addressing these issues. Israel is at the forefront of advances in ecological conservation through the development of solar-energy technologies, desalination, drip irrigation, water recycling, and electric-car infrastructure.

Core Concepts

- Israelis have developed innovative technologies to address the country's environmental issues.
- In keeping with the mitzvah of *bal tashḥit*, the Israeli government and Israeli non-profit organizations are dedicated to environmentalism, by planting trees, saving endangered species, and protecting natural resources.
- Israel's landscape and terrain are incredibly diverse for such a small country.
- Israel still faces ecological concerns, like water shortages and air and water pollution.

Learning Objectives – Students will:

- Cite Jewish sources about environmentalism, articulate the meaning of the Jewish mitzvah of *bal tashḥit*, and identify ways to perform the mitzvah. (Lesson 1)
- Articulate some of the environmental challenges facing Israel, and identify the root of these problems. (Lesson 2)
- Discuss some of the technological innovations Israel has developed to meet the environmental challenges facing it and the rest of the world. (Lesson 3)

Lesson Summaries

- Lesson 1: Students explore the mitzvah of *bal tashḥit*, discover how Israel practices it, and personalize it by making conservation posters for their synagogue/school.
- Lesson 2: Students have a fun competition to discover the root causes of Israel's environmental problems.
- Lesson 3: Students create mock talk shows, in which they interview conservation experts about Israel's environmental innovations.

Hebrew Connection

- **Bal tashḥit** –A mitzvah that requires us, as caretakers of the Earth, not to waste or destroy its resources. Lit. Do not destroy
- **Sh'mitah** – Leaving the land unplanted every seventh year

Tech Connection

- Visit Modern Israel Online with your class and explore the links for this chapter. Follow bird migration patterns in the Hula Valley, learn about salt-water irrigation and other efforts to tackle the water shortage, watch a video about a kibbutz that finds creative ways to support the environment, and more. See page 7 of this Lesson Plan Manual for more information about Modern Israel Online.
- Videotape your students conducting mock talk-show interviews with Israeli experts on conservation in Lesson 3, and post your videos to your class Wikispace.
- Visit the Jewish National Fund website at www.jnf.org to discover ways to help Israel tackle its environmental challenges.
- Invite students to make a list of ways congregants can get involved in environmental conservation locally, and post it to your Wikispace.
- Ask students to visit http://ecocamp.us/eco-footprint-calculator to calculate their own ecological footprint.

Chapter 7: Lesson 1

What is Jewish about environmentalism?

Materials Needed:

Poster board / construction paper, markers

Getting Started: (10 minutes)

Instruct students to work in *ḥevrutah* to complete the exercise **Judaism and the Environment** (page 77). Ask for volunteers to share their responses to the two questions posed: "In what ways does the Earth give to us?" and "In what ways can we give back to the environment?"

Exploring the Text:

1. (5 minutes) Discuss whether students feel that it is their responsibility to give back to the environment and take care of it. Direct students to the caption for the **palm trees photo** (page 76) and discuss how, for such a small country, Israel has a beautiful and diverse environment that needs to be protected.

2. (2 minutes) Point out that while Israel faces significant environmental challenges, it is at the forefront of ecological conservation and technological innovation. Israel's dedication to this comes from a Jewish mitzvah. Ask students to find the **name of the mitzvah** on page 86. (Bal Tashḥit, *which literally means "do not destroy"*)

3. (20-30 minutes) A student volunteer reads **Living Jewish Values** (page 86). Brainstorm ways to improve conservation at your synagogue / school. (*recycling plastic bottles during snack, shutting off the bathroom faucets, recycling paper in the synagogue offices, etc.*) Students make posters promoting these conservation ideas, using poster board and markers. Consider making the posters part of a campaign to "follow Israel's lead in environmentalism." Ask students to scan the chapter and add an explanation about how Israelis improve conservation for the issue their posters address.

4. (10 minutes, if time allows) Students "meet" Israeli environmentalists. Divide students into two groups. One group meets Sahar by reading **Meet an Israeli** (page 87). The other group meets Benjamin Kahn by reading the **coral reef caption** (bottom of page 86). Students choose one representative from each group to pretend to be Sahar and Benjamin, and tell the class about their environmental efforts.

Wrapping It Up: (5 minutes)
Option A: Ask: "How can we do a better job of *bal tashḥit* in our own lives?" Brainstorm some ways.
Option B: Complete the exercise **Your Turn: Water Use** (page 79). In this exercise, students determine how much water they use every day, compare with classmates, and answer: "How would your use of water change if you lived in Israel?"

Chapter 7: Lesson 2

What are some of Israel's environmental challenges?

Materials Needed:
Notebooks, pens / pencils

Getting Started: (3 minutes)
Students consider the **Debate It** question (page 85), and circle their choice of the two options. To help them develop their opinions, encourage them to read **Bringing back the swamp** (page 84).

Exploring the Text:

1. (12 minutes) Divide students into two groups based on their opinions on **Debate It** (page 85). Those who support draining the swamp to create farmland move to one side of the room, and those who support protecting the swamp move to the other side. Students debate the issue, using the debate format introduced in Chapter 4, Lesson 2. For 5 minutes, students compile their thoughts and shape an argument. Then, students debate for 5 minutes. Afterward, discuss how difficult it is to make decisions about how best to serve the community. Many nations struggle with these decisions, and Israel is no exception.

2. (30 minutes) Hold a competition to discover the root causes of Israel's environmental problems. In groups of three, students go section by section from **Solar energy** (page 78) through **Parks and wildlife** (page 84), and propose answers to the question: "What is a cause of the environmental problem addressed in this section?" For example, for the section **Desalination** (page 79), students can list: Israel is partially made up of desert, rain only falls in winter, the population's demand for water is increasing, etc. For every correct reason a group gives, it earns a point.

Wrapping It Up: (5 minutes)
Write the following five categories on the board: (1) Fossil-fuel conservation, (2) Water for drinking, (3) Water for agriculture, (4) Air pollution, (5) Wildlife protection and conservation. Assist students in dividing the environmental problems identified above into these categories. Note that Israel is at the forefront of advances in ecological conservation and that next week students will develop and present mock talk-show interviews in which they explore the innovative ways Israel is tackling these environmental issues.

Chapter 7: Lesson 3

How is Israel addressing its environmental challenges?

Materials Needed:

Video camera (optional), Israeli fruit (optional)

Getting Started: (2 minutes)

Remind students of Israel's five environmental challenges identified in Lesson 2. They are: fossil-fuel conservation, water for drinking, water for agriculture, air pollution, and wildlife protection and conservation. List them on the board.

Exploring the Text:

1. (20 minutes) Divide students into five small groups, assigning each group one of the environmental challenges. Each group will develop and rehearse a 3-minute mock talk-show interview with a fictional Israeli expert on its assigned issue. Students should refer to the appropriate pages of the text for information:
   a) Fossil-fuel conservation—**Solar energy** (page 78)
   b) Water for drinking—**Desalination** (page 79), **Cleaning up the water** (page 83)
   c) Water for agriculture—**Agriculture** (page 80), **Drip irrigation** (page 80), **Recycling water** (page 81)
   d) Air pollution—**Combating pollution** (page 82), **Air quality** (page 82)
   e) Wildlife protection and conservation—**Parks and wildlife** (page 84), **Bringing back the swamp** (page 84), **Protecting endangered species** (page 85), **Ruffling a few feathers** (page 85)

   Encourage students to be creative in naming their talk shows, as well as the hosts and guests. Tell them to make sure the interview covers the following questions:
   a) What is the major environmental challenge being addressed?
   b) How is Israel addressing it using conservation?
   c) How is Israel addressing it using innovation?
   d) What can Israeli citizens do to make a difference?

2. (23 Minutes) Each group presents its talk-show interview. Students review the content of each presentation by answering the questions above as a group. Consider filming the presentations and posting them to your class Wikispace. Optional: Distribute native Israeli fruit for students to snack on during the presentations (figs, dates, pomegranates, etc.).

Wrapping It Up: (5 Minutes)
Volunteers identify which Israeli environmental effort most fascinates and impresses them, and why.

CHAPTER

8 THE ECONOMY
Shekels and Cents

Chapter Overview: Students will learn about the evolution of Israel's economy as well as about some of the major advances made through Israeli ingenuity. Israel is rooted in socialist ideals, which gave birth to the kibbutz movement. The country has slowly moved more toward capitalism. Israel has been a leader in agriculture, fashion, research and development, and medicine. Israel has a successful economy, but it is not without its challenges. Israel works to address wealth gaps and low workforce participation through robust social programs.

Core Concepts

- Israelis have a strong sense of community responsibility, rooted in Jewish values and socialist ideals.
- Israeli technological ingenuity has yielded products that we use every day.
- An Israeli *shuk* is a unique shopping experience that is a clear representation of Middle Eastern culture.

Learning Objectives – Students will:

- Articulate how Israel's economy has changed and adapted since Israel's inception in 1948. (Lesson 1)
- Discuss what products and technological advances come from Israel. (Lesson 2)
- Describe what it is like to shop in an Israeli *shuk*. (Lesson 3)

Lesson Summaries

- Lesson 1: Through a fun Talmud exercise, students examine Israel's changing economy and develop a deep understanding of why Israel is committed to economic equality.
- Lesson 2: Students explore Israel's primary industries.
- Lesson 3: Students run a *shuk* experience for younger students in your school. Planning for the *shuk* begins at the end of Lesson 1 (or sooner, depending on the size and scope of your *shuk*). Consider involving parents in this project.

Hebrew Connection

- **Kibbutz**: A cooperative community in which each member contributes what he or she can, and in turn, receives what he or she needs
- **Shuk**: Outdoor Israeli market

Tech Connection

- Visit Modern Israel Online with your class and explore the links for this chapter. Imagine yourself on a kibbutz, learn about creative ways to help the needy, watch a video about a life-changing Israeli invention, and more. See page 7 of this Lesson Plan Manual for more information about Modern Israel Online.
- Ask a student to make a video tour of the *shuk* your class runs in Lesson 3.
- At the *shuk*, show any videos students have created throughout the year. You can also watch videos of famous *shuks* in Israel on Modern Israel Online.
- Create an "Internet cafe" at your *shuk*, where younger students visiting the *shuk* can explore the Israeli Embassy's kids page at http://www.israelemb.org/kids/.
- Have students visit the websites of various *kibbutzim* to find out their industries.

Chapter 8: Lesson 1

How has Israel's economy changed and adapted since the country's inception?

Materials Needed:
The worksheet with the *Pirkei Avot* quote, available at www.behrmanhouse.com/EMI, and a sample Talmud page, which you can find in the synagogue library, or by a simple online search for "Talmud page."

Getting Started: (5 minutes)
Ask students if they know what a kibbutz is. (*a cooperative community in which members contribute what they can, and in turn, receive what they need*) Then ask: "Would you like to live on a kibbutz? Why or why not?" Discuss the pros and cons of kibbutz life.

Exploring the Text:

1. (5 minutes) Brainstorm a list of the different jobs on a self-sufficient kibbutz. (*workers to run the kibbutz's industry as well as support roles: teachers, cooks, payroll, etc.*) Explain that *kibbutzim* grew out of Israel's socialist roots. Students work in *ḥevrutah* to define socialism, referring to the first paragraph on page 88. Discuss as a class.

2. (5 minutes) Explain that Israel began as a socialist society but has moved toward a capitalist economy. In *ḥevrutah,* students define capitalism, referring to **Move toward capitalism** (pages 88-89). Note that despite this shift, Israel maintains a strong sense of social responsibility.

3. (5 minutes) Give students a copy of the sample Talmud page. Explain that the Talmud page contains a Mishnah quote in the center with various commentaries by other sages below and around it, and that many voices contribute to the development of Jewish thought. In groups of three, students read **Back to the Sources** (page 91).

4. (10 minutes) Give each group the worksheet page with the text from *Pirkei Avot* 3:21 (referred to in **Back to the Sources**) in the center. Present the question, "Why does Israel try to have a strong economy in order to live up to this mishnah?" Students respond by writing in the spaces around the quote, like our sages did in the Talmud. Once students write an answer, you pass the page to another group who can either respond to the central quote, or to the response of the first group. (*Responses might include: It is important for Israel to live up to Jewish values; Jews have a communal responsibility to take care of Israel.*)

5. (5 minutes) Reflect on the Talmud exercise. Share the most compelling threads of thought. Ask: "What was it like doing this activity? Did any of your opinions change because of what a peer wrote?"

Wrapping It Up: (10 minutes)
Explain that Israel and Canada have a socialist health care system, controlled by the government. U.S. health care is controlled mostly by private companies. In 2010, the U.S. government passed legislation calling for more government involvement. Ask: "Why do you think it is important that citizens have access to health care? Does allowing equal and full access to health care live up to *Pirkei Avot* 3:21? How?"

Note: If your class is running a model *shuk* in Lesson 3, reserve some time in this class period for planning. For more details, see Lesson 3.

Chapter 8: Lesson 2

What are some of Israel's main economic sectors, and what are some of Israel's economic challenges?

Materials Needed:
Cell phones

Getting Started: (5 minutes)
Ask students to take out their cell phones and place them on their desks. As a class, discuss: "How do you or your family like having a cell phone? How is having a cell phone helpful?" Tell students that they can thank Israeli inventors for the cell phone; the technology was developed in Israel.

Exploring the Text:

1. (5 minutes) Explain that technology is only one sector of the Israeli economy. Have students look through the **industry subheads** (pages 94, 96, 98) to identify popular Israeli industries. *(Flowers/ agriculture, Fashion/textiles, Research and development, Medical advances, Tourism)* List them on the board.

2. (8 minutes) Divide the class into five groups, representing each of the industries listed on the board. Instruct each group to read the section labeled with its industry name (pages 94-99), highlight the industry's major points, and prepare a presentation. Direct the "Fashion/textiles" group also to read **Pioneering Spirit** (page 95) and both the "Medical advances" and "Research and development" groups to read **Cool Inventions** (page 97). Direct students to focus on at least one innovative product in the industry.

3. (12 minutes) Each group presents its findings. Discuss whether the Israeli industries presented are similar to or different from your local industries.

4. (10 minutes) After hearing about Israel's economic successes, ask students if they think Israel has any poor people. To find out, students silently read **Wealth gaps** (page 92). Ask: "How many Israelis live in poverty?" (*one out of four*) "Are you surprised? Why?"

5. In *ḥevrutah*, students read **Workforce** (page 92) to discover Israel's economic inequalities. Ask: "What are some of the inequalities? Are they similar to or different from economic inequalities in the United States and Canada? How?" Direct each *ḥevrutah* to continue reading **Helping the needy** (page 93). Ask: "What organizational structures are in place to make Israel a better place for all people?"

Wrapping It Up: (10 Minutes)
In *ḥevrutah*, ask students to read **Meet an Israeli** (page 93) and answer the questions at the bottom in which they plan a charitable organization. Then, ask each group to share its answers.

Note: If your class is running a model *shuk* in Lesson 3, reserve some time in this class period for planning. For more details, see Lesson 3.

Chapter 8: Lesson 3

What is a *shuk* like?

Note: This lesson follows a different format from the others in this Lesson Plan Manual. Below are detailed instructions for creating, designing, and implementing a *shuk* experience with your students for the children in the younger grades as well as for families and congregants. Start preparations a few weeks in advance of the event.

Two or Three Weeks Before

1. Before class, seek the permission of the education director to run a model *shuk*. Work with the director to secure a good location in the building for the *shuk*.
2. In class, read aloud **Outdoor Markets** (page 95). Tell students that they will create their own *shuk* for younger students in two weeks. Show more pictures or a video of a *shuk*, both accessible on Modern Israel Online.
3. Explain that *shuks* are a culturally significant part of Israeli culture, yet they are not the only way that Israelis shop. Israel has large shopping malls, grocery stores, corner stores, and general retail, similar to North America.
4. Assign roles for the *shuk*, and ask students to work on their *shuk* preparations at home. Most students will be vendors "selling" merchandise, such as baked goods, fruit, carrots and hummus, and handmade jewelry. They also can use fake merchandise as the basis for a game, like a ball toss at the pots-and-pan vendor. Other students can be street musicians, host a stand teaching about Israel (perhaps showing any videos students have created during the year), or run an Internet café featuring a computer station with the Israeli Embassy's kids website.
5. E-mail parents inviting them to the *shuk* and alerting them about any help or supplies needed. Enlist volunteers to help with setup and cleanup.
6. Invite the younger classes to your *shuk*. Consider having your students visit these classes to get younger students excited about the *shuk* experience.
7. Put a notice in your synagogue's e-newsletter inviting congregants to your model *shuk*.

One Week Before

1. Before class, design the setup of your *shuk* with your education director or synagogue administrator. Make sure that the custodial staff knows what supplies and setup are needed.
2. In class, remind students that next week the class will run a *shuk* for the younger students. Have the students start to create signs and decorations for the shuk which they can finish at home if they need more time; see if students have any questions; make sure they can secure needed materials; explain how the *shuk* will be laid out, etc. Remind students about the *shuk*'s atmosphere—that vendors often yell out to advertise their merchandise, and that customers and vendors often haggle over prices.

Shuk Day!

1. Set up the *shuk*. Decorate your *shuk* location; set out the merchandise, set up games, the computer, videos, etc.; musicians warm up.
2. Run the *shuk*! Have fun!

Wrapping It Up: (5 minutes)
Debrief the *shuk* experience. Did the students enjoy it? What did they learn about a *shuk*? How is a *shuk* different from the places we usually shop in the United States and Canada?

CHAPTER

9 CONNECTING WITH ISRAEL

Chapter Overview: This chapter summarizes what students have learned about Israel throughout the year. We follow the fictional character Justin as he takes us through the photographs from his trip. Justin is now aware of Israel's unique character and accomplishments as well as its challenges.

Core Concepts

- Knowledge about Israel is a critical part of what it means to be Jewish today.
- Travel to Israel is the best way to experience the intricacies and beauty of Israeli life, politics, and culture.
- Many fun opportunities exist for students to travel to Israel.
- Different locations in Israel offer varying tourist experiences that represent Israel's diversity of population, climate, geography, and more.

Learning Objectives – Students will:

- Appreciate the experiences of teens who have traveled to Israel on youth trips, and become excited at the prospect of traveling on these tours. (Lesson 1)
- Reflect on what they would like to experience in Israel, and come to their own understanding of different snapshots of life in Israel. (Lesson 2)
- Present their knowledge of various locations in Israel, utilizing the textbook and other resources to gather information. (Lesson 3)

Lesson Summaries

- Lesson 1: Guest speakers tell students about teen trips to Israel. Contact your local Jewish youth group to arrange speakers.
- Lesson 2: Students review what they have learned this year by labeling photographs of Israel, and by planning a brief presentation for the last class.
- Lesson 3: Acting as tour guides, students present research projects about Israeli locations, and have a *siyyum* celebrating the conclusion of the year.

Hebrew Connection

- **Siyyum**: Celebration for the culmination of a period of study or a unit of study

Tech Connection

- Visit Modern Israel Online with your class and explore the links for this chapter. Explore Israel in maps, watch a video about connecting with Israel, and more. See page 7 of this Lesson Plan Manual for more information about Modern Israel Online.
- Using Modern Israel Online, students develop a virtual tour of their assigned locations from Chapter 9: Lesson 3.
- View various promotional tour videos advertising teen trips to Israel.
- Create videos of the students acting as tour guides for various places in Israel as part of their Lesson 3 presentations. Consider posting these to your class Wikispace.

Chapter 9: Lesson 1

What travel opportunities to Israel are available for teens, and why should students consider participating in one of these tours?

Materials Needed:
Promotional material about trips to Israel, guest speaker (In advance of this lesson, contact your synagogue's youth director or a representative from your local affiliated Jewish youth group [BBYO, NCSY, NFTY, USY, Noar Chadash, etc.] and ask for the advisor and/or a student to make a presentation about trip options for teens.)

Getting Started: (5 minutes)
Explain to students that while it may be interesting and fun to learn about Israel in class, there is no substitute for traveling to Israel to experience it in person. As a group, discuss why this is so.

Exploring the Text:

1. (25 minutes) Invite a guest speaker (as described above) to talk about his or her group's trip options to Israel. Encourage students to ask questions about the tours.

2. (15 minutes) If possible, also invite a local teen who has traveled to Israel on a youth trip to talk about the experience and show trip photos. Students hear directly from a teen why he or she loved the trip, and ask questions about the experience.

Wrapping It Up: (5 Minutes)
Distribute promotional materials about youth trips to Israel, and discuss the importance of traveling to Israel. Discuss: "What excites you about the trips you heard about? What, if anything, makes you nervous?"

Chapter 9: Lesson 2

What have you learned this year?

Materials Needed:

Pencils, notebooks

Getting Started: (5 minutes)
Before class, write on the board: "What is the most interesting place in Israel to you, and why?" As students arrive, direct them to sit quietly and write their answers. They can flip through the entire book as a reminder.

Exploring the Text:

1. (5 minutes) Students share their responses to the opening question. Ask them to flip through **Chapter 9** (pages 100-104) to find out if Justin, a fictional character introduced in Chapter 1, picked the same locations. When a student finds one that matches, he or she shares what Justin said about it.

2. (25 Minutes) In *ḥevrutah*, students write their own captions for each of the pictures in the **Photo Album** (pages 100-104). Encourage them to discuss something that Justin left out. For example, for the picture at the top of page 102, they could write: "I was impressed by the talent and range of these musicians. They played a wide variety of music from both Jewish and Bedouin cultures." After students have written their captions, each group shares two of them with the class.

3. (5 minutes) With class input, make a list on the board of Israeli locations that students want to visit. For example, students might list Tel Aviv, the Old City of Jerusalem, Haifa, Eilat, the Negev Desert, the Golan Heights, etc. Have students fill in the locations in the **map of Israel** (page 105).

Wrapping It Up: (10 Minutes)
Assign each student a location to present about next week. Students are to become expert tour guides who will take the class on a 3-minute tour of the location. Encourage creative use of technology. Instruct students to thumb through their textbooks to find material, and to utilize the **Index** (pages 110-111). Students complete their research as homework. Advise them to use Modern Israel Online to gather information, and to refer to the **Resources** (page 107).
Optional: Students can create a virtual tour for their locations using Modern Israel Online. They can create a placemark for the location, and link related websites. Information about how to download and use Modern Israel Online is available at www.behrmanhouse.com/EMI.

Chapter 9: Lesson 3

What are the unique characteristics of various locations in Israel?

Materials Needed:
Israeli food, map of Israel, equipment needed for the presentations

Getting Started: (5 minutes)
Today is presentation day for the students. These 5 minutes allow students to ask you any final questions and prepare any media that they will be using.

Exploring the Text:

1. (30 minutes) Acting as tour guides, students give their presentations on Israeli locations. Be sure to have students locate their sites, either on the **map of Israel** (page 105), on a larger classroom map of Israel, or using the Google Earth environment of Modern Israel Online.

   Note: For larger classes, you may need to expand the time for this, and devote less time to "Wrapping It Up."

Wrapping It Up: (15 Minutes)
Students share something they learned about Israel this year that they found intriguing or surprising. Simultaneously, students eat the native Israeli food that you either ordered or made. Recipes for falafel, Israeli salad, and hummus are available in the "Arts and Culture" section of Modern Israel Online. This is your *siyyum* party to close the year.

Assessments and Additional Projects

There are a number of ways to assess your students' comprehension of the material presented in the text. Below, you will find both recall and open-ended questions as well as experiential project-based activities that you can use for each chapter to check that your students have internalized the material.

You may choose to add your own questions to the list based on the discussions and activities that are most successful in your classroom. You may also want to reformat these questions into multiple choice, or into a mixture of formats. To reinforce material and to encourage family learning, consider sending students home with a "car note," an index card with one of these questions on it each week. Using this strategy, students have something tangible to show their parents upon entering the car that will spark discussion about the lesson for the ride home.

Technology also offers exciting ways to assess your students' knowledge. Consider starting an online discussion board (possibly in a Wikispace) where students respond to a question each week. Encourage students to visit Modern Israel Online regularly to explore interesting links that relate to the topics under study. (See page 7 of this Lesson Plan Manual for more information about Modern Israel Online.) For more ideas on how to incorporate technology, check out the "Tech Connection" section at the start of each chapter in this Lesson Plan Manual.

Chapter 1: Introduction

1. Act out or write a text-message conversation between an American teen visiting Israel for the first time and her Israeli cousin. For example, the American might want to ask her cousin for advice about what she should pack for the trip.

2. Explain the difference between *Eretz Yisrael, Am Yisrael, and M'dinat Yisrael. (Eretz Yisrael = The Land of Israel. Am Yisrael = The people of Israel. M'dinat Yisrael = The State of Israel.)*

3. Name two facts about the Kotel. *(Answers may include: It is the holiest site for Jews; it is the site where the Temple once stood in Jerusalem.)*

4. Name two major biblical links to Israel that are discussed in the chapter. *(Israel is the land God promised to our ancestors. It is the land to which Moses led the Jewish people. It is the land where King Solomon built the Holy Temple.)*

5. Imagine you're traveling to Israel, and visiting the Kotel. Write a note to put in the Kotel.

6. How big is Israel? Visit Modern Israel Online and click on the "Directions" tab at the top left. Enter any two city names in Israel into the "From" and "To" fields and hit Enter. Scroll down to the bottom of the driving directions to see the total distance in driving time. Find the distances between different cities on the map. *(For example, Tzfat/Safed to Eilat is 5 hours 16 mins. Jerusalem to Tel Aviv is only 46 mins.)*

Chapter 2: Arts and Culture

1. In class, create an "Israeli restaurant," or take a field trip to a local one to sample Middle Eastern specialties such as Israeli salad, falafel, hummus, and shawarma. Write a restaurant review describing the food.

2. Brush up on your modern Hebrew with games on Modern Israel Online. You can find links in the "Sports and Games" placemark in this chapter.

3. Name three countries from which Jews emigrate to Israel. *(Russia, Poland, Yemen, Iraq, Ethiopia, the United States. Immigrants make aliyah to Israel from any place Jews live outside of Israel.)*

4. How are Israeli teens like or unlike American and Canadian teens? *(Israeli teens play sports, eat in restaurants, and go to the beach. Their food is somewhat different, their music is often in Hebrew or Arabic.)*

5. Visit Modern Israel Online and explore the music links for this chapter. Listen to a variety of music, then pretend that you are a music-review blogger and write a blog entry about an Israeli song. Write what you liked and didn't like, and compare the song to American music.

Chapter 3: A Diverse Nation

1. Play a game of "20 Questions" to test your knowledge about Israel's diverse population. Each student chooses a different cultural, religious, or immigrant group that lives in Israel. Classmates ask yes-or-no questions until they correctly identify the group.

2. What are two different ways that the word "*aliyah*" is used in Jewish life? *(Aliyah literally means "going up." It is the name used for being called up to the Torah, since it is a spiritually elevating event. It is also used for immigration to Israel. When Jews immigrate to Israel, it is called making aliyah, because moving to the Jewish holy land is considered a spiritual elevation.)*

3. Why is Israel's commitment to Jewish immigration so important to the Jewish people? Why would Israel enact a law like the Law of Return? *(To ensure that Jews have a safe place to go in case of anti-Semitism or persecution.)* You can read the full text of the Law of Return on Modern Israel Online, in the Jewish State chapter.

4. Visit Modern Israel Online and explore the culture or history of one of the major Jewish immigrant groups to Israel. Present your findings to the class. *(Yemenite, Russian, Ethiopian, and Anglo Jews)*

5. What other ethnic groups and religions call Israel home, and why? *(Christians, Christian Arabs, Muslim Arabs, Baha'i, Druze, and Bedouins)*

6. What problems could arise from having the Western Wall, Church of the Holy Sepulchre, and the Temple Mount so close to one another?

Chapter 4: A Jewish State

1. Do you think that "Hatikvah" is an appropriate national anthem for Israel? Why or why not? In English, write a new version of "Hatikvah" that accounts for all of the citizens of Israel, based on what you have learned in this chapter. You might want to set it to music and record yourself singing it. What might be gained by making these changes? What might be lost?

2. What are some of the challenges of building a coalition government in the Knesset? *(Parties need to work cooperatively to forge a coalition. Each party must make sacrifices, and work with others who they have disagreements with. Sometimes smaller parties have a disproportionately large amount of power.)*

3. Write a list of arguments for and against two of the three following statements:

    a) The Law of Return properly represents "who is a Jew."

    b) Orthodox citizens should be required to serve in the military like everybody else.

    c) Public buses should run on Shabbat in Israel.

4. Write your own opinion about two of the three statements above.

5. List two ways that the Israeli government is structured differently from the U.S. government. *(The head of the executive branch in Israel is called the prime minister; in the United States, it is the president. In Israel, there are many political parties; in the United States, there are two major parties. In the United States, citizens vote for candidates; in Israel, they vote for political parties. In the United States, there are two houses of Congress; in Israel, there is one, called the Knesset.)*

6. Take the "Volunteering in Israel" survey on Modern Israel Online, which you can find in the National Service placemark for this chapter. Create your own survey on volunteering in America or Canada and send it to ten friends, classmates, and/or family members. Compile the results and share them with the class. Do you notice any trends? What could the government or private organizations do to increase volunteerism?

Chapter 5: Layers of History

1. Using Modern Israel Online, create a placemark for a location in Israel, such as Tzfat (also called Safed), Jaffa, or Jerusalem, in which you trace its history from biblical times (if applicable) to today. Include links to photos, videos, and other historical information. Share your placemark with the class by saving your changes to the KMZ file, and e-mailing it or posting it to the class Wikispace.

2. Select and research an important figure from modern Israeli history. (Several are listed in this chapter.) Prepare a 3-minute presentation in which you take on the figure's persona. Using props, pictures, and notecards, introduce yourself to the class and talk about your life and your role in Israeli history.

3. Name three of the groups of people who controlled the Land of Israel, since the Second Temple was destroyed in the year 70 CE. *(Babylonians, Persians, Greeks, Romans, Ottomans, the British)*

4. Define the term "Diaspora." *(Any place that Jews live that is outside of Israel.)*

5. Explain the Uganda Plan. If you were Theodor Herzl, would you have accepted this proposal? *(The Uganda Plan offered the Jewish People a homeland in Uganda instead of in the Land of Israel.)*

6. Pick one event from the online timeline that the class created—other than the event you researched—and explain it in as much detail as you can.

Chapter 6: Security and Conflict

1. Develop an idea for a program that promotes peace by getting Israeli and Palestinian teens to interact. Create a flyer or a video promoting the program.

2. Name two groups of people who are exempt from serving in the Israel Defense Forces. *(Religiously observant women, Arab Israelis, yeshiva students, physically handicapped individuals)*

3. Why is military service compulsory in Israel?

4. When it comes to politics and the peace process, are you more of a "hawk" or a "dove"? Why?

5. Visit Modern Israel online and locate the West Bank, the Gaza Strip, and the Golan Heights. Click on the Ruler icon at the top of the screen to measure the distances between these areas and major cities in Israel. What do the distances tell you about the need for peace in the region? *(Israel's neighbors are very close, and peace is urgently needed to maintain Israel's security.)*

6. Controversy exists over Israel's security fence and security checkpoints. Pick one of these two controversial security measures, and list two pros and two cons.

Chapter 7: The Environment

1. Bumper stickers are a popular way for Israelis to express their diverse opinions. Design three bumper stickers about Israeli environmental issues.

2. Pretend you are the manager of a plant in Tel Aviv that makes chocolate sauce. A new Food Network show is coming to interview you about the ways in which your business has become more environmentally friendly. Using the material in the chapter, act out the interview with a partner.

3. Explain the mitzvah of "*Bal Tashḥit*." List two ways you can incorporate this mitzvah into your life. (Bal Tashḥit *literally means "do not destroy." It is the mitzvah that drives us to take care of the environment. Examples include conserving water and recycling paper.)*

4. How would your use of water change if you lived in Israel?

5. If you had lived in Israel in the 1950s, would you have supported draining the Hula Valley swamp to create more farmland? Why or why not?

6. Pick one of the five environmental challenges identified in this chapter—other than the one you were assigned to research—and answer these three questions:

    a) How is Israel addressing the challenge using conservation?

    b) How is Israel addressing the challenge using innovation?

    c) What can Israeli citizens do to make a difference?

Chapter 8: The Economy

1. Based on what you have learned about Israel, create a fictional Israeli company in one of the industries described in the chapter *(Flowers/agriculture, Fashion/textiles, Research and development, Medical advances, Tourism).* Prepare a presentation about the company, and design an advertisement. Address these questions: What is your product or service? Who founded the company and what's their background (are they *olim*, sabras, etc.)? What Jewish value does your company hold central to its operation? Why and how?

2. Name two things you think the younger students learned by visiting your *shuk*.

3. Explore the kibbutz-related links for this chapter on Modern Israel Online. Using the "Fly to" tab, locate some of the *kibbutzim* mentioned in the textbook chapter or in the links on Modern Israel Online. Define what a kibbutz is, and list some of the jobs required for a kibbutz to run effectively. *(A kibbutz is a cooperative community in which each member contributes what he or she can and in turn receives what he or she needs. Jobs include workers to run the kibbutz's industry as well as support roles: child care, teachers, cleaners, cooks, payroll, etc.)*

4. Give two examples of how the Israeli economy has shifted from its socialist roots toward capitalism. *(Businesses are owned by private individuals, not the government. The government has privatized many companies it used to own like the phone company and El Al airlines.)*

5. How are the economic challenges in Israel similar to or different from those in the United States? *(Similarities include the existence of poverty in both countries and the large wealth gaps between rich and poor. Differences include the fact that many* ḥaredi *men in Israel do not work but devote their lives to Torah study, and unemployment is high among Arabs for a variety of reasons.)*

Chapter 9: Connecting with Israel

1. Be a tour guide! Using Modern Israel Online, create a virtual tour for a trip to Israel. Create placemarks for major cities and places of interest in Israel and label each of them with one or two facts that you would tell your tour group. Share your tour with the class by e-mailing the KMZ file or posting it to the class Wikispace.

2. What are some advantages to traveling to Israel with peers on organized teen tours? *(You get to experience Israel with friends, you have programs tailored to your age group, they tend to last a number of weeks, funds are often available to help pay for them, they are a lot of fun!)*

3. What is the most interesting place you learned about in Israel, and why?